W9-CAD-772

Smart Ways to Spend Your Time

The Constructive Use of Time Assets

by Pamela Espeland and Elizabeth Verdick

free spirit
PUBLISHING®

Helping kids
help themselves™
since 1983

MAY 06

Library of Congress Cataloging-in-Publication Data
Espeland, Pamela.
    Smart ways to spend your time : the constructive use of time assets / by Pamela Espeland and Elizabeth Verdicl
      p. cm. — (The "Adding assets" series for kids; bk. 4)
    Includes index.
    ISBN 1-57542-172-0
 1. Leisure—Juvenile literature. 2. Recreation—Juvenile literature. 3. Children—Time management—Juvenil
literature. I. Verdick, Elizabeth. II. Title.
    GV182.9.E76 2005
    790'.083'4—dc22   200402334

Search Institute℠ and Developmental Assets™ are trademarks of Search Institute.

The original framework of 40 Developmental Assets (for adolescents) and the Developmental Assets fc Middle Childhood were developed by Search Institute © 1997 and 2004, Minneapolis, MN; 1-800-888-782 *www.search-institute.org*. Used under license from Search Institute.

The FACTS! (pages 8, 27, 44, and 61) are from *Coming into Their Own: How Developmental Assets Promote Positiv Growth in Middle Childhood* by Peter C. Scales, Arturo Sesma Jr., and Brent Bolstrom (Minneapolis: Searc Institute, 2004).

Illustrated by Chris Sharp
Cover design by Marieka Heinlen
Interior design by Crysten Puszczykowski
Index by Ina Gravitz

10 9 8 7 6 5 4 3 2 1
Printed in the United States of America

Free Spirit Publishing Inc.
217 Fifth Avenue North, Suite 200
Minneapolis, MN 55401-1299
(612) 338-2068
help4kids@freespirit.com
www.freespirit.com

Contents

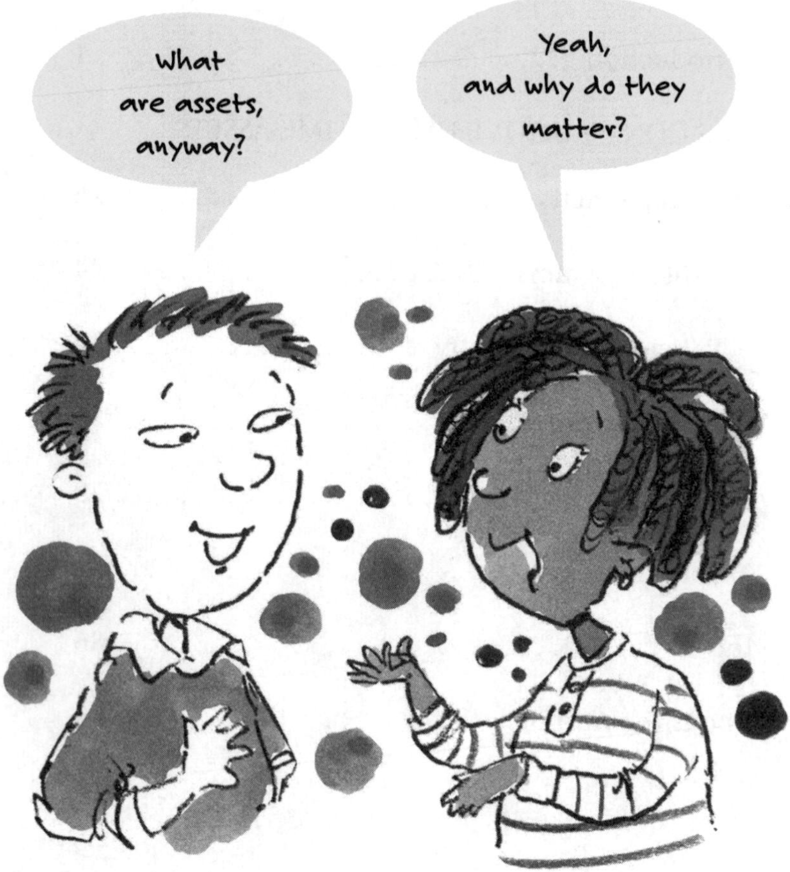
What are assets, anyway?
Yeah, and why do they matter?

Introduction

If you knew ways to make your life better, right now and for the future, would you try them?

We're guessing you would, and that's why we wrote this book. It's part of a series of eight books called the **Adding Assets Series for Kids.**

What Are Assets, Anyway?

When we use the word **assets**, we mean good things you need in your life and yourself.

We don't mean houses, cars, property, and jewelry—assets whose value is measured in money. We mean **Developmental Assets** that help you to be and become your best. Things like a close, loving family. A neighborhood where you feel safe. Adults you look up to and respect. And (sorry!) doing your homework.

There are 40 Developmental Assets in all. This book is about adding four of them to your life. They're called the **Constructive Use of Time Assets** because they're about spending your free time in positive, healthy ways. They're about having fun and interesting things to do—on your own, with your friends, with your family, and with other grown-ups who care about kids. When you have these assets, you're hardly ever bored. You have hobbies. You like to learn and do new things. You're active and creative and full of ideas.

The Constructive Use of Time Assets

Asset Name	What It Means
Creative Activities	You do something with music, art, drama, or creative writing two or more times a week.
Child Programs	You go to an organized after-school activity or community program for kids two or more times a week.
Religious Community	You go to a religious program or service once a week or more.
Time at Home	On most days, you spend some time with your parents. You spend some time doing things at home besides watching TV or playing video games.

Other books in the series are about the other 36 assets.* That may seem like a lot, but don't worry. You don't have to add them all at once. You don't have to add them in any particular order. But the sooner you can add them to your life, the better.

---

* If you're curious to know what the other assets are, you can read the whole list on pages 80–81.

Why You Need Assets

An organization called Search Institute surveyed hundreds of thousands of kids and teens across the United States. Their researchers found that some kids have a fairly easy time growing up, while others don't. Some kids get involved in harmful behaviors or dangerous activities, while others don't.

What makes the difference? Developmental Assets! Kids who have them are more likely to do well. Kids who don't have them are less likely to do well.

Maybe you're thinking, "Why should I have to add my own assets? I'm just a kid!" Because kids have the power to make choices in their lives. You can choose to sit back and wait for other people to help you, or you can choose to help yourself. You can also work with other people who care about you and want to help.

Many of the ideas in this book involve working with other people—like your parents, grandparents, aunts, uncles, and other family grown-ups. And your teachers, neighbors, coaches, Scout leaders, and religious leaders. They can all help add assets for you and with you.

It's likely that many of the adults in your life are already helping. In fact, an adult probably gave you this book to read.

How to Use This Book

Start by choosing **one** asset to add. Read the stories at the beginning and end of that chapter. The stories are examples of the assets in everyday life. Then pick **one** idea and try it. See how it goes. After that, try another idea, or move on to another asset.

Don't worry about being perfect or getting it right. Know that by trying, you're doing something great for yourself.

The more assets you add, the better you'll feel about yourself and your future. Soon you won't be a kid anymore. You'll be a teenager. Because you have assets, you'll feel and be a lot more sure of yourself. You'll make better decisions. You'll have a head start on success.

We wish you the very best as you add assets to your life.

Pamela Espeland and Elizabeth Verdick
Minneapolis, MN

A Few Words About Families

Kids today live in many different kinds of families.

Maybe you live with one or both of your parents. Maybe you live with other adult relatives—aunts and uncles, grandparents, grown-up brothers or sisters or cousins.

Maybe you live with a stepparent, foster parent, or guardian. Maybe you live with one of your parents and his or her life partner.

In this series, we use the word **parents** to describe the adults who care for you in your home. We also use **family adults**, **family grown-ups**, and **adults at home**. When you see any of these words, think of your own family, whatever kind it is.

Creative Activities

Sanjay's Story

Sanjay has always loved music, ever since he got his first toy piano when he was only two. Now he has electronic keyboards in the basement, and he spends a lot of his free time making up his own songs. He also takes piano lessons once a week, so he's learning harder songs and new skills.

When his friends come over, they like to go down in the basement with him and check out his family's CD collection. There's all kinds of music, from classical to jazz to rock, folk, country, rap, R&B, alternative, and even his stepmom's "easy listening."

Today, it's a sunny summer afternoon, but Sanjay is indoors. He's tinkering with some new electronic gear his dad picked up for him at the secondhand music store. Some of Sanjay's friends show up outside the basement's sliding glass door, where they all start knocking at once. "Come out, Sanj, we're going to have a water-balloon fight!"

Sanjay looks up and sees Kari, Mike, Jamie, and Tyrell. They're all in bathing suits, standing in the blazing sun. Sanjay likes his friends a lot, but he's really into what he's doing right now. All day, he's been sampling parts of songs from the CD collection and recording them.

"They're going to think I'm a loser if I don't join them," he thinks. "But I'm not ready to stop."

Still, he knows he can't ignore his friends when they're standing right there on the doorstep, wanting to have some fun.

Sanjay has the *Creative Activities* asset, and he's trying to figure out how to make time for his friends, too.

Think about your own life. Do you spend time each week on activities that spark your creativity?

If **YES**, keep reading to learn ways to make this asset even stronger.

If **NO**, keep reading to learn ways to add this asset to your life.

You can also use these ideas to help add this asset for other people—like your

Facts!

Kids with the *Creative Activities* asset:

✓ have higher self-esteem

✓ do better in school

✓ get along better with others

friends, family members, neighbors, and kids at school.

ways to Add This Asset

 **AT HOME**

Look into Lessons. Acting, dancing, singing, drawing, painting, music, photography—whatever you like, give it a try. You think you *might* like it but you're not 100 percent sure? Try it anyway. Talk to a family grown-up about your interest, then ask for help finding a teacher. *Examples:* You might try guitar lessons, sign up for dance at a local center, join the choir at your place of worship, or check out a community theater program for youth.

TiP: No money for lessons? Maybe one of your neighbors teaches piano. Ask if you can trade lawn mowing for lessons. No piano at home to practice on? Maybe there's one at your school you can use, if you get permission. Or maybe there's one at your place of worship. Or maybe a friend's family has a piano. If you want something badly enough, you can find a way!

Don't Give Up. Lessons aren't for everyone, and they aren't always a big success. Maybe you fell in love with the trombone and talked your parents into buying you one. You didn't like the first lesson, and you *hated* the second one. And the sounds that came out of your trombone were simply awful—like a cow mooing. Hey, it happens. Don't beat yourself up, and don't give up. Maybe two weeks isn't enough to decide what to do. Are you willing to give it another two weeks, or four? Maybe you need to find another instrument—one that's right for you. Everyone's good at something. And even if you're not the best musician in the world, you can still enjoy making music of your own. Blow into a harmonica or tap out some rhythms on whatever you have handy: blocks of wood, buckets, old pots and pans (ask your parents which ones you can use).

Don't Expect Perfection. So what if your photographs aren't always in focus, or if you do your best singing in the shower. Big deal if you color outside the lines or get stuck trying to write a rhyme. Teacher, author, and all-around creative person Mary Lou Cook once said, "Creativity is inventing, experimenting, growing, taking risks, breaking rules, making mistakes, and having fun." Good advice!

A message for you

What if you feel a little silly every time you practice your pliés or rehearse your raps? That's natural when you're trying something new. What if you have a sibling who's a gifted artist or a star in the choir and gets a ton of attention? You can still do your own creative activities. (You might have an easier time—and more fun—because the spotlight isn't on you.)

Creative activities aren't about impressing other people. They aren't always about performing. They can be things you do to please *yourself*. *P.S.* In case you're wondering, a *plié* is a ballet move.

Be Creative at Home. You don't always need a teacher to help you express your creativity. There's a lot you can do on your own. *Examples:* Instead of plunking down in front of the TV, grab a pencil and paper and sketch a self-portrait. If you have colored pencils or crayons, draw your own comic book. Check out a book on *origami* (Japanese paper-folding) from the library and give that a try. Get some old magazines, scissors, and glue and make a collage. Write a short story or make up a song. Snap some photos with a disposable camera. If your family has a video camera (and your parents let you use it), shoot a home video.

Get Artsy with Your Family.
Have a family meeting to talk about ways to experience the arts together. Check your local newspaper for ideas. Do museums have family nights? Are there free concerts in the park? Is a favorite author giving a reading at a bookstore? Can you go to a play or musical at the high school? Is a new gallery opening nearby? Make a date once a month (or more often) to do something artsy as a family. Give everyone a chance to choose.

TiP: You can also enjoy the arts together at home. Listen to music. Read poetry. Watch a movie version of a play. Read a play out loud, with everyone taking a different part. Check out art books from the library and look at them together. Look at museum Web sites on the computer. (Want to visit the famous Louvre Museum in Paris? Go to *www.louvre.fr*.) Work on a family project—like a scrapbook or a video. What else can you think of to do together?

Support Each Other's Creative Activities. Is your brother in a band? Is your dad an amateur actor? Does your sister sing in a choir? Show your support by going to each other's performances and events. Invite friends and other family members to come along.

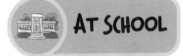 **AT SCHOOL**

★ Does your school offer classes, clubs, and after-school programs in music or the arts? If it does, you're lucky. Many schools don't. Take advantage of these opportunities while you have the chance.

★ Stick up for arts education. Do you think it's important to learn about music, art, and drama in school? Write letters to your principal, members of your school board, your city council, and your state lawmakers and tell them how you feel. If your school has classes and programs in the arts, say thank you. If it doesn't, explain in a letter that you want some. If your friends feel the same way you do, have them sign your letter, too.

★ Take part in your annual school talent show, art show—or both. If your school doesn't have these events, talk with a teacher about how to start them.

★ A science fair is another way to be creative at school. You might have a great idea for a project, or you might make a special display. Since science fairs have rules you need to follow, check with your teacher first.

8 Ways the Arts Are Great for You

1. The arts make you smarter. They build all kinds of thinking skills.

2. Creative writing helps you become a better writer and builds your vocabulary.

3. Acting makes you a better reader and speaker.

4. Music builds math skills.

5. The arts build life skills like patience, persistence, problem-solving, and positive risk-taking.

6. You learn self-confidence, social skills, and a sense of identity.

7. Experiencing art from different cultures builds tolerance, respect, and *empathy* (the ability to understand how other people feel).

8. Art makes life more interesting and fun.

And those are just for starters.

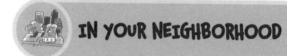

IN YOUR NEIGHBORHOOD

★ Support the arts in your neighborhood or community. Go with your parents or other family grown-ups to local concerts, plays, openings, and recitals. (Many are free.) Check out museums and galleries. (Most galleries are always free; many museums have free days.) Coffee shops often show art by local artists. Ask a parent if you can stop in, take a look—and have a cup of cocoa while you're there.

★ Have a neighborhood talent show in someone's backyard or a nearby park. Not just for kids—include grown-ups, too. Maybe someone's mom plays the saxophone. Or someone's uncle knows magic tricks. Suggest that people bring snacks to share after the show.

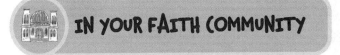

IN YOUR FAITH COMMUNITY

★ Does your faith community have a children's choir, chorus, band, or liturgical dance group? If not, see if you can start one. Or ask if kids can join adult groups—if not all the time, then for special services or occasions. *P.S.* In case you're wondering, *liturgical dance* is an expression of prayer and worship through movement. It is sometimes called *praise dance, sacred dance,* or *praise and worship dance.*

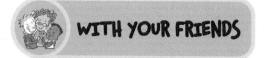

WITH YOUR FRIENDS

★ Instead of just hanging out together, do something creative. What about making a movie? Maybe one of you has and knows how to use a video camera. Or come up with a comedy routine or joke show, then perform it for younger kids. Or maybe you could get your parents' permission to paint a mural in your bedroom or on a basement wall.

★ Explore the arts as a group. Attend each other's school concerts or plays, if you go to different schools. Visit a museum together.

TiP: If you're going to a museum, call ahead and see if you can get a *docent*—a specially trained tour guide—to show you around. Or, if that's not possible, see if you can bring along some extra money to rent headphones that explain the exhibits.

Start Adding!

Pick at least ONE idea you've read here and give it a try. Then think about or write about what happened. Will you try another way to make creative activities a regular part of your life?

Back to Sanjay's Story

Sanjay goes to the door and invites his friends in.

"Whoa," says Tyrell, "it's totally dark in here! What are you, a vampire or something?"

"Come out and play, Count Dracula," Jamie adds with a laugh.

"Wait, check this out, guys," says Sanjay. "I've got bits and pieces of all kinds of stuff here. Listen up and see if you recognize anything."

He starts to play the samples he's recorded. His friends quiet down and listen, figuring the water balloons can wait.

After a few minutes, Kari says, "I just heard some OutKast in there."

"Yeah, and Smashmouth, and ABBA," Jamie adds.

"And James Brown!" says Tyrell. "My mom *loves* James Brown."

"Dude, did I just hear some, uh, Barry Manilow?" asks Mike, looking at Sanjay like he's gone a little crazy. "Have you turned into my grandpa or something?"

His friends laugh. Then they tease Sanjay some more about being a vampire—a super old one with weird taste in music.

Sanjay smiles. "Hey, don't knock it. Barry Manilow can really play piano."

"You're always saying stuff like that, Sanj," Kari chimes in. "But you know what? I think it's great. Every time we come over, it's like going to a music library or something."

"Yeah," adds Mike, "you've got tunes here that most kids at school wouldn't ever think of listening to. It's cool that you do your own thing."

"Okay, whatever!" Jamie exclaims. "NOW can we go outside?"

Everyone laughs, and Sanjay goes upstairs to grab his swim trunks. He's glad he has friends like them.

Child Programs

Erika's Story

Erika loves her Girl Scout troop, and she's been with the same core group of girls for two years in a row. In their small town, Erika, Abbie, Maria, and Jen are the only girls in their troop, so they call themselves the "Fab Four." This doesn't mean they're a clique or anything, though. They love telling other girls about Scouts and encouraging them to join, too.

But a lot has changed for Erika in the past few months. Her parents have separated and are planning to get divorced. Her dad has moved into an apartment across town, and her mom is working a full-time job. Sometimes her mom has to work nights.

These days, Erika is being shuffled back and forth between her parents. Almost every morning, she wakes up and thinks, "I wish it was all just a bad dream!"

Lately, she's missed some Girl Scout meetings because neither of her parents can give her a ride. Erika knows she could ask one of her friends for a ride, or even their troop leader, Ms. Martinez. But that would mean telling them why she needs a ride, and she's not ready to do that.

How can she possibly explain about the divorce? So she makes up excuses for not going, like "I'm sick," or "I have too much homework," or "I have an important family event to go to."

It feels icky to lie to Ms. Martinez and her friends, but Erika doesn't know what else to do.

The phone rings. It's Jen. "Hi, Erika," she says. "What's up? Don't forget about tomorrow's meeting, okay? We have all sorts of stuff to talk about: the father-daughter dance, the overnight, and volunteering at the food shelf. You'll be there, right?"

"Yeah, um . . . ," Erika stammers, "I don't know—I feel like I'm getting a headache, and I don't know if I'll be able to come." Of course, it's a lie, but she can't seem to stop herself.

Erika has the *Child Programs* asset, but her life is changing, and she's not sure how everything fits together anymore.

Think about your own life. Do you spend a few hours each week in organized activities with other kids? Are you in sports, a club, or another after-school program?

If **YES,** keep reading to learn ways to make this asset even stronger.

If **NO,** keep reading to learn ways to add this asset to your life.

Facts!

Kids with the *Child Programs* asset:

✔ **have stronger social skills**

✔ **are less likely to get into trouble**

✔ **are better readers**

You can also use these ideas to help add this asset for other people—like your friends, family members, neighbors, and kids at school.

ways to Add This Asset

 **AT HOME**

Get Busy! No matter what time of year it is, you can get involved in *something.* How about a school sports team? (Today, find out when the next tryouts are.) A community club? (Tonight, ask a family adult to help you find a program that interests you—anything from sports to volunteering. Then make a plan to call for more information.) Or what about the kids' program in your faith community? (If you haven't joined already, ask your dad or mom for help signing up.)

Ask What Others Are Doing. Think about your friends. They probably don't all live in your neighborhood, go to your school, and do the same things you do. What kinds of activities and programs are they involved in? Call or email them to find out. Do they like the activities and programs? Do they like the other kids who go? What new skills and talents have they learned? Is there anything they do that you'd like to try?

PSSSSSST....

This book is about adding assets to your life. If you want to add a *lot* of assets all at once, start with *Child Programs*—the asset you're learning about right now. Getting involved in an organized after-school activity or community program for kids is one of the *best* things you can do for yourself.

Ask What Others Have Done. Do you have older brothers or sisters? What kinds of activities and programs were they in when they were your age? Do your friends have older siblings? Talk with them, too. Are there teenagers you know in your apartment building or neighborhood? Ask for their ideas and advice.

Start a Club at Home. Maybe you're already involved in child programs a couple times a week, but you want *more*. Get a parent's permission to start a club that meets at your house once a week, or a few times each month. Clubs can be about anything: books, sports, collections, stickers, music, computers, pets, hobbies, or just hanging out as a group.

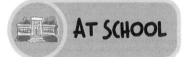

AT SCHOOL

★ Find out what your school offers. There may be clubs, organizations, or activities you haven't even heard of yet. Maybe you could make a list of all the choices at your school. Ask permission to post it on the bulletin board so other kids can read it, too.

★ If you join an after-school program, plan to stick with it for a while, even if you don't love it right away. Some kids drop out of programs too soon, or skip around to different programs without giving any of them a real chance. Suppose you sort of like a program you're in, but parts of it could be more fun. Why not tell the leader of the program? Come up with some helpful suggestions for improvement.

> **TIP:** When you talk to the leader, start by saying something good about the program. Then it won't sound like you're just complaining. *Example:* Don't say this: "Mr. Mack, we only play volleyball two times a week! Why can't we play every day?" Say this instead: "Mr. Mack, I really like it when we play volleyball. It's fun! Do you think we could do it more than two times a week?"

★ If you're not excited by anything your school offers right now, start something new. Find 5–10 other kids who share your interest. Get together and talk about the kind of group you'd like to start. What would be its purpose? What would be your goals? What kinds of things would you do? Write down your ideas. Then talk with a teacher or school counselor. Ask him or her to be your sponsor or recommend someone else who might do this. *P.S.* In case you're wondering, a *sponsor* is a responsible adult who will help you start your group and keep it going.

9 Fine Reasons to Join a Program for Kids

You'll . . .

1. have a safe place to go

2. have fun and interest-
   ing things to do

3. meet new people
   and make new
   friends

4. get to know adults
   who care about kids

5. learn positive values

6. build your self-esteem

7. learn new skills

8. learn more about yourself

9. feel good about how you're spending
   your time

★ Want to have fun *and* make a difference? Join a service club at your school. If your school doesn't have a service club, see if you can start one. Call or visit other schools in your community to learn what kids there are doing. Or ask your friends, if they go to different schools. You might suggest starting a Kids Care Club. Clubs must be sponsored by a school, church, synagogue, community center, or other youth organization. To learn more, visit this Web site: *www.kidscare.org.*

IN YOUR NEIGHBORHOOD

★ Many community programs for kids have a sports focus. Sports help you build your skills, smarts, and self-confidence. They're a great way to exercise and get in shape. Sometimes community sports programs aren't as competitive as school programs. This means that more kids can join, and you don't have to worry so much about how athletic you are. See what teams are available in your town or city. Check out your local park or community center. What about the YMCA or YWCA?

IN YOUR FAITH COMMUNITY

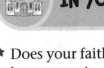

★ Does your faith community have organized activities or programs for kids your age? If it does, get involved. If it doesn't, ask if the adult leaders might be willing to sponsor a program or give one a home.

> **TiP:** Many Scout troops are sponsored by faith communities. These troops hold their meetings in churches, synagogues, or mosques.

WITH YOUR FRIENDS

★ Things are more fun when you do them with your friends. They're also less scary at the start. Find a friend who wants to get involved in an after-school activity or community program. Then join together. *P.S.* In the beginning, you and your friend may mostly hang out together at the activity or program. But remember that it's fun to get to know other people, too. This is a great way for both of you to meet and make new friends.

5 Positive Programs for Kids

1. **Camp Fire USA.** Fun programs and services for boys and girls build caring, confident youth and future leaders. *www.campfire.org*

2. **Boy Scouts of America.** Character development and leadership training for boys and young men. *www.scouting.org*

3. **Girls Incorporated.** Programs that inspire all girls to be strong, smart, and bold. *www.girlsinc.org*

4. **Girl Scouts of the USA.** Builds character and skills for success in girls and young women. *www.girlscouts.org*

5. **Police Athletic Leagues (PAL).** Athletic, recreational, and educational activities for kids. *www.nationalpal.org*

Start Adding!

Pick at least ONE idea you've read here and give it a try. Then think about or write about what happened. Will you try another way to get involved with after-school activities and community programs?

Back to Erika's Story

"Erika, what's up with you?" Jen asks. "You're always saying you're sick. Everyone's wondering what's going on. Ms. Martinez says she might call your mom to find out why you're missing meetings."

Erika doesn't want that to happen—not yet. "Oh, uh, Jen, my dad just walked in. Gotta run," she lies, then hangs up the phone.

The next day, her mom picks her up after school and says, "Good news—I can drop you off at Scouts on my way to work, and your dad can pick you up after and take you to his apartment. So you won't have to miss your meeting."

Erika makes up another lie. "The meeting got canceled. Ms. Martinez has the flu."

"That's too bad," her mom says. "I know how much you love Scouts. We'll just go home then."

As soon as they get home, Erika plops down on the couch and starts to cry. "Mom! It's not true about Ms. Martinez being sick, okay? The Scouts are meeting right now, and I just don't want to go. They'll ask me a bunch of questions about why I've been missing meetings. I don't want to tell anyone about our family. No one will understand!"

Erika's mom sits down beside her and says, "I think your Scout troop *would* understand. Listen, I'm going to call in to work and tell them I'm going to be late. You and I need to talk."

As Erika's mom goes to use the phone, the doorbell rings. When Erika answers it, she's surprised to see Ms. Martinez and the Fab Four.

"We're the Get Well Party!" they all say at once.

Erika is speechless.

"We understand if this isn't a good time," Ms. Martinez says kindly. "But if you want some company, we're here for you."

"Wow," Erika says, "this is a surprise . . . but a good one!" She stands there smiling.

"Aren't you going to let us in?" Ms. Martinez asks with a laugh.

Erika opens the door wide and yells, "Mom! Guess who's here?"

As the group files in, Maria announces, "We took a vote and decided that if you couldn't be at the meeting, we'd try to bring the meeting to you." She pulls cookies, lemonade, and paper cups from a cooler and puts them on the coffee table.

Erika's mom walks into the room. "Well, hello to all of you!" she says.

"I hope you don't mind us just showing up like this," Ms. Martinez replies. "We'll only stay a few minutes. We're here to remind everyone that being a troop means more than doing fun activities—though those are important! Being a troop means being there for each other in good times and bad. Right, girls?"

"Right!" the troop echoes.

"Okay, I get it," Erika says. "And I've really missed you all." She looks at her mom and asks, "Can they stay a while? And, Mom, can we tell them what's really going on?"

"Of course," her mom smiles. "But only if you pass me a cookie first!"

Religious Community

Rob's Story

Rob is at his locker on Friday when his new friend Tony asks if he can do a sleepover on Saturday. "It'll be fun," Tony says. "We can skateboard, and play computer games, and stay up really late watching a movie. My dad lets me stay up on Saturday nights because we sleep in on Sundays."

"Cool," says Rob, "I'll ask my parents. But there's just one thing: On Sunday mornings, we always go to early service at our church."

"Can't you skip it just this once?" Tony asks. "It will be more fun if we can stay up late. Last week, my friend down the street stayed over, and my dad ordered a pizza at midnight. Maybe he'll do that again."

"I don't know . . . I guess I'll have to think about it," Rob says. "I'm pretty sure my parents won't want me to miss church."

Actually, Rob isn't sure *he* wants to miss church. Wendy, his Sunday-school teacher, is like the big sister he never had, and most of the kids in the class are really nice. Rob enjoys the singing parts of the service, and he looks forward to a late breakfast at a restaurant with his family afterward.

In fact, early service on Sunday feels like a habit, one that's comfortable and familiar. It's hard to explain that to other kids sometimes.

"Hey, Tony," he says, "I have to catch my bus. But I'll call you tonight about Saturday.

As he heads for the bus, Rob wonders what he should do. "Tony's fun," he thinks, "and I'd like to get to know him better. Maybe I can skip church this once."

Rob has the *Religious Community* asset, and he feels lucky that he does.

Think about your own life. Do you go to a religious program or service at least once a week? Maybe more?

If **YES,** keep reading to learn ways to make this asset even stronger.

If **NO,** keep reading to learn ways to add this asset to your life.

You can also use these ideas to help add this asset

Facts!

Kids with the *Religious Community* asset:

✓ get along better with their parents

✓ feel more connected to their community

✓ have a stronger sense of well-being

for other people—like your friends, family members, neighbors, and kids at school.

ways to Add This Asset

AT HOME

Talk About the Big Questions. Like most kids, you're full of questions about life. And not just little questions, but BIG ones: Where do we go when we die? What does God or the Creator look like? What is spirituality, and why does it matter? Why do bad things sometimes happen? Are all of our prayers answered—why or why not? Share these questions with your parents and other family adults. They may not have all the answers, but they can help you better understand your family's beliefs—and guide you as you form your own.

Practice What You've Learned. At your church, temple, meeting house, or mosque, you learn about the beliefs and values of your religion. At home, you can practice what you've learned. *Examples:* Treat your family with love and respect. Help out around the house. Be peaceful with your siblings instead of fighting. Say a prayer of thanks for all you have.

Lead the Way. What if your family doesn't have a faith community? If you're interested in religious services or spiritual activities, talk with your parents or other adults in your family.

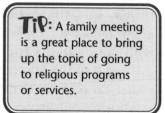

TiP: A family meeting is a great place to bring up the topic of going to religious programs or services.

See if they might be willing to start going with you to religious programs or services. If they're not interested or not ready, maybe you can join a friend's faith community. Or maybe you can go to services or meetings with another relative or a family friend.

5 Good Things
About Religious Communities

Religious communities . . .

1. teach values. Values help kids make good choices and decisions.

2. are usually safe, supportive places to be.

3. can be great places to meet lots of different people. Young, old, and in-between, with all kinds of interests and skills.

4. care about young people. They want them to succeed and stay out of trouble.

5. are smart places to go for help and answers.

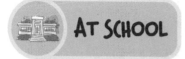

AT SCHOOL

★ Unless you go to a private religious school, your school community and your religious community can seem like two different worlds. That doesn't mean you can't live by your values and beliefs at school (or anywhere else). Let them guide you to do and be your best.

★ Sometimes, school events and religious events conflict. Talk with your parents about which to choose. Which seems most important to you and other people? *Examples:* If you have a big part in the school play, you may have to skip the scavenger hunt at your temple. If you're singing a solo with your church choir, you may need to miss the school party.

IN YOUR NEIGHBORHOOD

★ Different religious communities have different beliefs. Some of those may seem strange or wrong to you. Talk this over with your parents and religious leaders. They will probably encourage you to respect different beliefs, even if you don't agree with them. When people don't respect each other's beliefs, this can lead to prejudice, discrimination, violence, hate crimes—even wars. Set a good example for others to follow. Be tolerant and accepting.

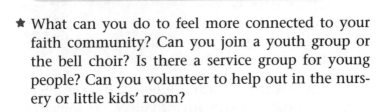

IN YOUR FAITH COMMUNITY

★ What can you do to feel more connected to your faith community? Can you join a youth group or the bell choir? Is there a service group for young people? Can you volunteer to help out in the nursery or little kids' room?

★ Does your faith community sometimes have special services for kids and teens? If it does, be sure to go and take part. If it doesn't, maybe you can help put one together.

★ Do you need help with a problem in your life? Is there a question that's driving you crazy? Something you just don't understand? Look around your faith community. Chances are, there are plenty of people you can talk to or ask for advice—people who share your values and beliefs. What about your youth leader? A clergy person? A teacher? The music director? Who else?

> **TIP:** Your faith community may be the only place you spend time (outside your family) where people really talk about their values and beliefs. Sometimes you need adults in your life who will say, "This is right," or "That is wrong," *and* give you good reasons for *why.* Your faith community is a great place to find them.

WITH YOUR FRIENDS

★ Don't give each other a hard time for going to church, synagogue, temple, meetings, or mosque. Respect each other's beliefs. You might go as a group to events and activities in each other's faith communities. Before you go, ask if there are certain ways you should dress or behave. *Examples:* Girls might have to cover their hair, or sit apart from boys and men. You might be expected to sit in complete silence for a period of time. Or you might be invited to dance and sing with music, or share greetings with other worshippers during the service.

Start Adding!

Pick at least ONE idea you've read here and give it a try. Then think about or write about what happened. Will you try another way to make religious community a bigger part of your life?

Back to Rob's Story

Rob gets home from school and heads into the kitchen for a snack. His grandpa, who lives in a small apartment above their garage, is waiting for him, like he always is.

"Ice cream again?" Rob asks.

"Gotta keep this body in shape," Grandpa answers, patting his belly and smiling. "Grab the scoop and dig in. Here's an apple for you, too—Mom's orders."

"Thanks, Grandpa," Rob says, joining him at the table. "I have to ask you something. My friend Tony asked me to sleep over Saturday and skip church the next morning. I want to go to his house—but I don't want to miss Sunday school or church or our family breakfast. What should I do?"

"Hmmm . . . ," Grandpa replies. "Who says you can't do it all? Spend the night, but bring your good clothes and get up early. We'll pick you up on the way."

"Yeah, but Tony wants to stay up real late, and I'll be tired. He thinks it's fun to be up all night and stuff."

"I've got an idea," Grandpa says. "How about inviting Tony to join us? If he's going to come along, he might not want to stay up so late the night before."

"But I don't even know if we're the same religion."

"Well, that's a good point," says his grandpa. "But look at it this way: It's a chance for him to get to know our family better, and to try something a little different one time. There's no harm in asking. But if Tony says no, that's okay, too. It's a decision that's completely up to him and his family."

"And if he says no, I'll have to decide if I want to stay over or not, and if I want to stay up late or not," Rob says.

"That's a lot to decide," Grandpa says, smiling. "You'll probably want to talk it over with your mom and dad."

"But first, I'll ask them if it's okay to bring Tony along on Sunday."

"That sounds like a plan," Grandpa answers. "Now you'd better finish your ice cream before it melts."

Later that night, Rob calls Tony to find out if he's open to the idea. "The best part is Sunday school, because we do fun activities and stuff," Rob explains. "The other kids are pretty cool, too. And then after church we go to this awesome restaurant where you can order any kind of pancakes in the world."

"Okay, I'm up for it," Tony agrees. "Hold on while I ask my dad."

Time at Home

What it means: On most days, you spend some time with your parents. You spend some time doing things at home besides watching TV or playing video games.

Ona's Story

Ona yells, "I'm home!" at the top of her lungs, says a quick hi to her dad and her sister Kim, and dashes to her room. "Practice ran late—sorry!"

As she digs through her dresser drawers, she hears Mom come into the apartment and say, "I smell wontons! And I really worked up an appetite in rush hour."

"Hurray, it's clean!" Ona thinks while pulling out her favorite striped nightshirt. She puts it on, along with her slippers, and heads into the kitchen. She kisses her dad on the cheek and peers into the wok. "Looks yummy," she says. Both her dad and her big sister Kim are wearing pajamas, too.

"I'm making the noodles, Mom's in charge of rice, and you get to set the table," Kim says. Ona holds back from calling her "Miss Bossy." After all, it's Family Friday, and she doesn't want to spoil the fun.

Mom walks into the kitchen wearing her blue robe. "Hugs all around," she says, and everyone embraces her.

"I pick *Clue* tonight," Ona announces as she puts bowls on the table.

"You always pick *Clue*," Kim says, rolling her eyes.

"Well, I suppose you're choosing some dumb card game," Ona answers in a huff.

"Girls!" their dad warns. But he doesn't look angry. In fact, he looks happy as he tosses the vegetables—and sort of silly, Ona has to admit, in his purple PJs and apron. It's all part of their Friday night tradition: pajamas, dinner together, and a whole night of playing games. Each person gets to choose one game, and everyone else has to be a good sport about it. The TV stays off, and no videos or computers are allowed, either.

As Ona sets the last of the silverware, the doorbell rings. She looks out the peephole and sees Carmen standing in the hall. Carmen is a girl who lives in the apartment below them. She and Ona play together sometimes. Right now, Carmen is wearing mismatched pajamas and a big grin.

"Uh-oh, Mom, Dad," Ona says, "I think we've got company. . . ."

> **Ona has the *Time at Home* asset, and it's one of her favorite things.**

Think about your own life. Do you spend time at home with your family doing fun and creative things together? Do you do things at home besides watch TV, play video games, or zone out in front of the computer?

Facts!

Kids with the *Time at Home* asset:

✓ do better in school

✓ get along better with their friends

✓ get along better with their families

If **YES**, keep reading to learn ways to make this asset even stronger.

If **NO**, keep reading to learn ways to add this asset to your life.

You can also use these ideas to help add this asset for other people—like your friends, family members, neighbors, and kids at school.

Ways to Add This Asset

AT HOME

Eat Dinner Together as a Family. With everyone's busy schedule, you might not be able to do this every night. But do it as often as you can. Over and over, studies show that the *more* often kids eat dinner with their families, the *less* likely they are to smoke cigarettes, drink alcohol, or use illegal drugs. Plus kids who eat dinner with their families are *less* stressed, *less* bored, and *more* likely to get good grades in school. They have better vocabularies and healthier eating habits, too. Wow! All that, just for eating dinner together!

Make Family Time Count. After long days at school and work, many families can barely squeeze in dinner, homework, and all the other "have-to" stuff. Before you know it, it's time for bed. Here are some ways to fit in a little extra family fun: Read one chapter of a book together. Laugh at the comics and do some puzzles in the newspaper. Play a quick game of catch. Walk the dog. Talk about your day. All those moments will add up.

Have a Family Project or Hobby. Choose something that's fun for everyone (and one you can set aside and come back to often). *Examples:* scrapbooking, jigsaw puzzles, or a family newsletter you send out every month or so to faraway grandparents, aunts, uncles, and cousins.

8 More Ways to Have Fun at Home with Your Family

1. Rent a funny movie. Make pizza or popcorn and watch it together.

2. Listen as everyone plays one favorite song or CD. If it makes you feel like dancing, dance!

3. Camp out together in the backyard, basement, or family room.

4. Plant a garden together. Each person gets a section, a row, or a pot on the balcony or windowsill.

5. Play games together—simple ones like *Candyland* or *Chutes and Ladders* if there are very young children in your family, harder ones like *Monopoly* or *Scrabble* or *Trivial Pursuit* if everyone is older.

6. Cook a special dinner together. Let each family member fix one special dish. What if you end up with a weird mix of tacos, fish sticks, Jell-O, and bologna sandwiches? One time won't matter.

7. Check out tapes or CDs of old-time radio shows from the library—ones your grand-parents or other relatives probably loved long ago. Like *Jack Benny* or *Dragnet* or *The Shadow*. Turn the lights down low and gather around the stereo or boombox to listen.

8. Create a comic book about your family. Everyone gets to add a page or a story.

Spend Your Alone Time Well. When you're feeling bored and no one's around, it's easy to turn on the TV or veg out with a video game. These activities are fine once in a while, but not if that's *all* you do. Try being creative and using your imagination. *Examples:* Build a model, draw a picture, play outside, work on a collection, write a story, sing, dance, or just daydream.

Get Interested in Your Family. You've got lots to think about and do, and sometimes it's easy to forget about the people you live with every day. Make an effort to show interest in what they're thinking and doing, too. *Example:* "Hey, Mom, what's that magazine you're reading? It looks cool." *X-Treme example:* Hang out with your sister or brother for an hour, doing whatever she or he wants to do—even if it's something you think is boring or babyish. It might be more fun than you expect.

Read. Curl up in a comfy chair or a corner of the sofa and read whatever looks fun or interesting. Save homework reading for another time—this is just for you. If you're not sure what to read, ask a teacher, librarian, or media center person for ideas. They will *love* the chance to help you find something you want to read.

Appreciate Your Family. What do you like best about your mom? Your dad? Your baby sister? Can you think of at least *three* things you like about everyone you live with? Maybe you can name ten or more. Now, what's *one* thing that makes each person unique? Interesting? Especially lovable?

TiP: Turn this into a family activity. Each family member writes down three things they like about one other family member, and one thing that makes that person unique.

Have Regular Family Meetings. They're a great way to stay in touch, solve problems, and get everyone involved in family decisions. If your family doesn't have regular family meetings, ask your parents if they're willing to give it a try.

6 Tips for Terrific Family Meetings

1. Set a starting time, ending time, and place for your meeting. *Example:* Every Thursday after dinner, from 7:00–7:30, at the kitchen table.

2. A few days before the meeting, put a piece of paper on the kitchen counter. Have family members write down things they want to talk about during the meeting. Bring the paper to the meeting. Use it as your *agenda*— your list of things to talk about and do.

3. Agree on a few simple ground rules in advance. *Examples:* Everyone gets a chance to talk. Everyone listens respectfully when someone else is talking. No whining or raised voices.

continued

4. Decide on a leader for each meeting. Everyone should get a chance to lead—not just the grown-ups.

5. Take turns talking. You might pass around a "talking stick." The person holding the stick gets to talk without being interrupted. A talking stick can be almost anything— a chopstick, a ruler, a wooden spoon. Or your family might want to make a fancy decorated talking stick.

6. Try to end the meeting on time so it doesn't drag on and on.

Treat Your Family with Kindness and Respect. Use your *best* manners, not your *worst* manners. *Examples:* Say "please" and "thank you." Chew with your mouth closed. If you want something, ask nicely instead of whining or yelling. Listen when other people talk. Don't snoop, lie, interrupt, swear, or take each other's stuff without asking. Want to know more? Go to the library and check out a book on etiquette (a fancy word for manners).

At School

★ Each day, store away at least *one* thing to tell your family about school. Maybe the lasagna at lunch was gross. Maybe science class was cool. Or maybe your principal got the hiccups during morning announcements. Whatever it is, when your parents ask, "What happened in school today?" you'll have something to say!

★ Some kids do too many after-school activities, which keeps them away from home too much. Other kids don't do enough. Try to find a balance in your life. Ask a parent or other family adult for help.

> **TiP:** Remember that *Child Programs* is an asset you want to add. This means going to an organized after-school activity or community program for kids two or more times a week. If you don't know about this asset yet, see pages 24–40.

IN YOUR NEIGHBORHOOD

★ With your family, think of another family in your building or neighborhood that you'd like to know better. Invite them to dinner and see how it goes. If you all get along, think of other ways to spend time together. Maybe you could go to a movie or the park. Maybe you could have a picnic together or even take a day trip together sometime. These are all great ways to build an "extended family" when your relatives live far away.

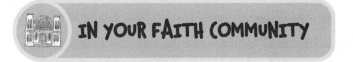

IN YOUR FAITH COMMUNITY

★ With your youth group or religion class, brainstorm ideas for things families can do together. Write them down. Post them on the bulletin board or ask if they can be published in the worship bulletin.

★ For many people, their faith community is a "home away from home." Families spend time together worshipping, doing service activities, volunteering, or working for peace. Does your faith community feel this way to you? Talk this over with your family. Are there ways you can get more involved?

WITH YOUR FRIENDS

★ Invite friends to spend time with you and your family. Do this as often as you can. Help them to feel like part of your family. Maybe they'll do the same for you. Then you'll all have more than one family.

TIP: If you know someone who's in a not-so-good home environment, make a special effort to reach out. Making that person part of your family could change his or her life.

A message for you

For some kids, home is not a good place to be. Maybe their families fight a lot. Or they don't feel safe at home. Or nobody else is ever around and they're left alone most of the time. If your home seems unhappy or unhealthy to you, try to spend more time in positive places. Sign up for after-school activities or community programs for kids, if you can. Hang out at friends' homes where people treat each other with respect (and the parents or other family adults are present). Find a place where you feel safe and welcome—and don't give up until you do.

Start Adding!

Pick at least one idea you've read here and give it a try. Then think about or write about what happened. Will you try another way to make your time at home better, more satisfying, and more fun?

Back to Ona's Story Ona isn't sure what to do, since Family Friday is supposed to be for family only. "Mom!" she whispers. "Carmen's standing out there like she's ready to join us. She's even wearing pajamas! I told her about our Fridays, but I didn't invite her over!"

"Well," her mom answers, "we can't leave her standing in the hall in that strange get-up, can we?"

Ona opens the door. "Hi, Carmen. Come on in."

"Hi there, Carmen," Ona's mom says, smiling. "We're just sitting down to dinner. Would you like to join us?"

"Yes, thank you," Carmen says.

Ona and her sister look at each other in surprise. Their parents have always made it clear that Friday nights are for the family. It's hard to believe they're breaking their own rule like this.

"Set another plate, please, Ona," says their dad.

During dinner, Ona's parents ask Carmen the usual questions—how she likes school, what activities she's involved in, how her family is doing. Ona is surprised when Carmen remarks, "On Friday nights, both my parents work really late, and I used to have a babysitter, but now I stay home alone because I'm old enough. But I'm not scared or anything."

"Let's give one of them a call after dinner so they know where you are, okay?" Ona's mom suggests.

Ona reaches for another wonton and looks sideways at Carmen. "I wouldn't want to be all alone every Friday night," she thinks to herself. "And I bet it *does* get scary sometimes, no matter what Carmen says."

After everyone has finished eating, Carmen jumps up to clear the dishes. "No, no," says Ona's dad, "please sit down. You're our guest, and the rule is that guests and the head cook—and that's me tonight—get to sit and talk while everyone else cleans up. Now, Carmen, tell me: What's your favorite game?"

Ona smiles and catches Mom's eye. "Thanks, Mom," she says quietly. "You and dad are the best."

A NOTE TO GROWN-UPS

Ongoing research by Search Institute, a nonprofit organiza-tion based in Minneapolis, Minnesota, shows that young people who succeed have specific assets in their lives—**Developmental Assets** including family support, a caring neighborhood, integrity, resistance skills, self-esteem, and a sense of purpose. This book, along with the other seven books in the **Adding Assets Series for Kids,** empowers young people ages 8–12 to build their own Developmental Assets.

But it's very important to acknowledge that building assets for and with young people is primarily an *adult* responsibility. What kids need most in their lives are grown-ups—parents and other relatives, teachers, school administrators, neighbors, youth leaders, religious leaders, community members, policy makers, advocates, and more—who care about them as individuals. They need adults who care enough to learn their names, to show interest in their lives, to listen when they talk, to provide them with opportunities to realize their potential, to teach them well, to give them sound advice, to serve as good examples, to guide them, to inspire them, to support them when they stumble, and to shield them from harm—as much as is humanly possible these days.

This book focuses on four of the 40 Developmental Assets identified by Search Institute. These are **External Assets**—positive experiences kids receive from the world around them. The four external assets described here are called the **Constructive Use of Time Assets.** They're partly about spending time alone in positive, creative ways (not in front of the TV!). But they're mostly about spending time with caring adults in organized, structured activities and programs.

These adults devote their time, efforts, energy, and experience to teaching music, art, drama, and creative writing—and to running supervised programs for kids in communities, in churches and synagogues and mosques, in schools and parks and wherever they can find the space. They make an enormous difference in the lives of countless children. Three of the four Constructive Use of Time assets rely on their commitment and dedication. Yet we don't want our kids to spend all of their time in activities and programs away from home. The fourth asset, Time at Home, calls for *daily* quality time with parents, and *daily* time spent well at home, alone or with family members.

What all children need is a *balance* of scheduled and free time. Interaction time and alone time. Planned time and staring-into-space time. A healthy community offers kids a variety of constructive, engaging activities—and also leaves room for daydreaming.

A list of all 40 Developmental Assets for middle childhood, with definitions, follows. If you want to know more about the assets, some of the resources listed on pages 84–85 will help you. Or you can visit the Search Institute Web site at *www.search-institute.org*.

Thank you for caring enough about kids to make this book available to the young person or persons in your life. We'd love to hear your success stories, and we welcome your suggestions for adding assets to kids' lives—or improving future editions of this book.

Pamela Espeland and Elizabeth Verdick
Free Spirit Publishing Inc.
217 Fifth Avenue North, Suite 200
Minneapolis, MN 55401-1299
help4kids@freespirit.com

The 40 Developmental Assets for Middle Childhood

EXTERNAL ASSETS

SUPPORT

1. **Family support**—Family life provides high levels of love and support.
2. **Positive family communication**—Parent(s) and child communicate positively. Child feels comfortable seeking advice and counsel from parent(s).
3. **Other adult relationships**—Child receives support from adults other than her or his parent(s).
4. **Caring neighborhood**—Child experiences caring neighbors.
5. **Caring school climate**—Relationships with teachers and peers provide a caring, encouraging school environment.
6. **Parent involvement in schooling**—Parent(s) are actively involved in helping the child succeed in school.

EMPOWERMENT

7. **Community values children**—Child feels valued and appreciated by adults in the community.
8. **Children as resources**—Child is included in decisions at home and in the community.
9. **Service to others**—Child has opportunities to help others in the community.
10. **Safety**—Child feels safe at home, at school, and in her or his neighborhood.

BOUNDARIES AND EXPECTATIONS

11. **Family boundaries**—Family has clear and consistent rules and consequences and monitors the child's whereabouts.
12. **School boundaries**—School provides clear rules and consequences.
13. **Neighborhood boundaries**—Neighbors take responsibility for monitoring the child's behavior.
14. **Adult role models**—Parents(s) and other adults in the child's family, as well as nonfamily adults, model positive, responsible behavior.
15. **Positive peer influence**—Child's closest friends model positive, responsible behavior.
16. **High expectations**—Parent(s) and teachers expect the child to do her or his best at school and in other activities.

CONSTRUCTIVE USE OF TIME

17. **Creative activities**—Child participates in music, art, drama, or creative writing two or more times per week.
18. **Child programs**—Child participates two or more times per week in cocurricular school activities or structured community programs for children.
19. **Religious community**—Child attends religious programs or services one or more times per week.
20. **Time at home**—Child spends some time most days both in high-quality interaction with parent(s) and doing things at home other than watching TV or playing video games.

COMMITMENT TO LEARNING

1. Achievement motivation—Child is motivated and strives to do well in school.

2. Learning engagement—Child is responsive, attentive, and actively engaged in learning at school and enjoys participating in learning activities outside of school.

3. Homework—Child usually hands in homework on time.

4. Bonding to adults at school—Child cares about teachers and other adults at school.

5. Reading for pleasure—Child enjoys and engages in reading for fun most days of the week.

POSITIVE VALUES

6. Caring—Parent(s) tell the child it is important to help other people.

7. Equality and social justice—Parent(s) tell the child it is important to speak up for equal rights for all people.

8. Integrity—Parent(s) tell the child it is important to stand up for one's beliefs.

9. Honesty—Parent(s) tell the child it is important to tell the truth.

10. Responsibility—Parent(s) tell the child it is important to accept personal responsibility for behavior.

11. Healthy lifestyle—Parent(s) tell the child it is important to have good health habits and an understanding of healthy sexuality.

SOCIAL COMPETENCIES

12. Planning and decision making—Child thinks about decisions and is usually happy with the results of her or his decisions.

13. Interpersonal competence—Child cares about and is affected by other people's feelings, enjoys making friends, and, when frustrated or angry, tries to calm herself or himself.

14. Cultural competence—Child knows and is comfortable with people of different racial, ethnic, and cultural backgrounds and with her or his own cultural identity.

15. Resistance skills—Child can stay away from people who are likely to get her or him in trouble and is able to say no to doing wrong or dangerous things.

16. Peaceful conflict resolution—Child attempts to resolve conflict nonviolently.

POSITIVE IDENTITY

17. Personal power—Child feels he or she has some influence over things that happen in her or his life.

18. Self-esteem—Child likes and is proud to be the person he or she is.

19. Sense of purpose—Child sometimes thinks about what life means and whether there is a purpose for her or his life.

20. Positive view of personal future—Child is optimistic about her or his personal future.

Helpful Resources

Books

Create! A Sketchbook and Journal (San Francisco, CA: Chronicle Books, 2001). Invites kids to sketch, write, draw, paste, and create any way they want. Spiral-bound book comes with a set of eight colored pencils.

Free to Be You and Me: And Free to Be...a Family (25th Anniversary Edition) by Marlo Thomas (Philadelphia, PA: Running Press, 1998). Stories, songs, poems, and pictures in a fun-filled book for kids and their families.

Reaching Your Goals by Robin Landew Silverman (New York: Franklin Watts, 2004). To turn a wish into a goal takes creative thinking and organized planning skills. This book shows how to make a plan and see it through to the end.

The Kids' Multicultural Craft Book: Creative Activities from 30 Countries by Roberta Gould (Charlotte, VT: Williamson Publishing, 2004). Historical information and instructions for how to create craft projects from cultures around the world. This book can keep you busy for hours.

Making Things: The Handbook of Creative Discovery by Ann Sayre Wiseman (Boston: Little Brown & Company, 1997). Ideas for fun and easy crafts like candles, weaving, sculptures, kites, and more. Also includes advice for what to do when a project doesn't turn out as you'd hoped.

The Mudpies Book of Boredom Busters by Nancy Blakey (Berkeley, CA: Ten Speed Press, 1999). Outdoor activities, rainy day projects, things to do in the kitchen, and on-the-road travel games.

Web sites

Family Games
www.familygames.com
A great place to find fun, nonviolent games, quizzes, and software. Downloads are available plus links to more games, riddles, puzzles, and activities the whole family can enjoy.

Class Brain
www.classbrain.com
Brain games, word puzzles, homework help, and creative project ideas. There's also an action adventure arcade and strategy tips for different board and card games.

Fun Brain
www.funbrain.com
Games are sorted by grade (K–12), and categories include things like Math Baseball, Funbrain Arcade, Grammar Gorillas, One False Move, Dare to Be Square, and more. Also searchable by subject: Geography, Art, Languages, Math, Music, Science, and Technology.

National Youth Leadership Council (NYLC)
www.nylc.org
The NYLC brings kids, educators, and community leaders together to make sure that kids are seen, heard, and actively involved in community organizations and decision making.

FOR ADULTS

Books

Building Assets Is Elementary: Group Activities for Helping Kids Ages 8–12 Succeed by Search Institute (Minneapolis: Search Institute, 2004). Promoting creativity, time-management skills, kindness, manners, and more, this flexible activity book includes over 50 easy-to-use group exercises for the classroom or youth group.

More Than Just a Place to Go: How Developmental Assets Can Strengthen Your Youth Program by Search Institute (Minneapolis: Search Institute, 2004). Helps youth programs integrate the Developmental Assets into their programs. Includes examples from successful and diverse programs. Companion to the 29-minute VHS video of the same title.

What Kids Need to Succeed: Proven, Practical Ways to Raise Good Kids by Peter L. Benson, Ph.D., Judy Galbraith, M.A., and Pamela Espeland (Minneapolis: Free Spirit Publishing, 1994). More than 900 specific, concrete suggestions help adults help children build Developmental Assets at home, at school, and in the community.

What Young Children Need to Succeed: Working Together to Build Assets from Birth to Age 11 by Jolene L. Roehlkepartain and Nancy Leffert, Ph.D. (Minneapolis: Free Spirit Publishing, 2000). Hundreds of practical, concrete ideas help adults build Developmental Assets for children in four different age groups: birth to 12 months, ages 1–2, 3–5, and 6–11. Includes inspiring true stories from across the United States.

Web sites

Alliance for Youth
www.americaspromise.org
Founded after the Presidents' Summit for America's Future in 1997, this organization is committed to fulfilling five promises to American youth: Every child needs *caring adults*, *safe places*, a *healthy start*, *marketable skills*, and *opportunities to serve*. This collaborative network includes resources, information, and opportunities for involvement.

Connect for Kids
www.connectforkids.org
Tips, articles, resources, volunteer opportunities, and more for adults who want to improve the lives of children in their community and beyond. Includes the complete text of Richard Louv's book *101 Things You Can Do for Our Children's Future.*

A Game a Day
www.agameaday.com
Puzzles, word games, and brain teasers that encourage creative thinking and build problem-solving skills. Recommended by the American Library Association, appropriate for ages 9 and up.

National Mentoring Partnership
www.mentoring.org
The organization provides connections, training, resources, and advice to introduce and support mentoring partnerships. The site is a wealth of information about becoming and finding a mentor.

Search Institute
www.search-institute.org
Through dynamic research and analysis, this independent nonprofit organization works to promote healthy, active, and content youth and communities.

Index

About the Authors

Both Pamela Espeland and Elizabeth Verdick have written many books for children and teens.

Pamela is the coauthor (with Peter L. Benson and Judy Galbraith) of *What Kids Need to Succeed* and *What Teens Need to Succeed* and the author of *Succeed Every Day*, all based on Search Institute's concept of the 40 Developmental Assets. She is the author of *Life Lists for Teens* and the coauthor (with Gershen Kaufman and Lev Raphael) of *Stick Up for Yourself!*

Elizabeth is a children's book writer and editor. She is the author of *Teeth Are Not for Biting, Words Are Not for Hurting,* and *Feet Are Not for Kicking* and coauthor (with Marjorie Lisovskis) of *How to Take the GRRRR Out of Anger* and (with Trevor Romain) of *Stress Can Really Get on Your Nerves* and *True or False? Tests Stink!*

Pamela and Elizabeth first worked together on *Making Every Day Count*. They live in Minnesota with their families and pets.

More Titles in the Adding Assets Series for Kids

By Pamela Espeland and Elizabeth Verdick. Each book is for ages 8–12. *Each $9.95; softcover; two-color illust., 5⅛" x 7".*

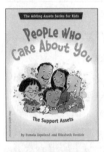

People Who Care About You
Kids learn how to build the six Support Assets: Family Support, Positive Family Communication, Other Adult Relationships, Caring Neighborhood, Caring School Climate, and Parent Involvement in Schooling. Stories, tips, and ideas bring them closer to their families and strengthen other important relationships in their lives. *96 pp.*

Helping Out and Staying Safe
Kids learn how to build the four Empowerment Assets: Community Values Children, Children as Resources, Service to Others, and Safety. Stories, tips, and ideas guide them to play useful roles at home and in the community, help others, and feel safer at home, at school, and in their neighborhood. *80 pp.*

Doing and Being Your Best
Kids learn how to build the six Boundaries and Expectations Assets: Family Boundaries, School Boundaries, Neighborhood Boundaries, Adult Role Models, Positive Peer Influence, and High Expectations. Stories, tips, and ideas show them why and how boundaries help them behave in positive, responsible ways. *96 pp.*

Other Great Books from Free Spirit

Our Family Meeting Book
Fun and Easy Ways to Manage Time,
Build Communication, and Share Responsibility
Week by Week
by Elaine Hightower and Betsy Riley
Family meetings are proven ways to involve
everyone in planning, solving problems, and
staying close. This inviting book makes fam-
ily meetings manageable, meaningful, and enjoyable for everyone.
With 52 agendas full of original photographs and eye-catching
illustrations (featuring many write-on pages), it's a planning tool
that becomes a history of family life—and a treasured keepsake.
For parents.
$16.95; 136 pp.; softcover; color photos & illust.; lay-flat binding; 9" x 9"

The Kid's Guide to Service Projects
Over 500 Ideas for Young People Who Want to Make
a Difference
by Barbara A. Lewis
Projects range from simple things anyone can do
to large-scale commitments that involve whole
communities. Choose from a variety of topics
including animals, crime, the environment,
literacy, and politics. "Service Project How-Tos"
offer step-by-step instructions for creating flyers, petitions, and
press releases; fundraising; and more. For ages 10 & up.
$12.95; 184 pp.; softcover; 6" x 9"

*To place an order or to request a free catalog of SELF-HELP FOR
KIDS® and SELF-HELP FOR TEENS® materials, please write, call,
email, or visit our Web site:*

Free Spirit Publishing Inc.
217 Fifth Avenue North • Suite 200 • Minneapolis, MN 55401-1299
toll-free 800.735.7323 • local 612.338.2068 • fax 612.337.5050
help4kids@freespirit.com • www.freespirit.com

Fast, Friendly, and Easy to Use
www.freespirit.com

Browse the catalog

Info & extras

Many ways to search

Quick check-out

Stop in and see!

Our Web site makes it easy to find the positive, reliable resources
you need to empower teens and kids of all ages.

The Catalog.
Start browsing with just one click.

Beyond the Home Page.
Information and extras such as links and downloads.

The Search Box.
Find anything superfast.

Request the Catalog.
Browse our catalog on paper, too!

The Nitty-Gritty.
Toll-free numbers, online ordering information, and more.

The 411.
News, reviews, awards, and special events.

 Our Web site is a secure commerce site. All of the personal
information you enter at our site—including your name,
address, and credit card number—is secure. So you can
order with confidence when you order online from Free Spirit!

For a fast and easy way to receive our practical tips, helpful information,
and special offers, send your email address to upbeatnews@freespirit.com.
View a sample letter and our privacy policy at *www.freespirit.com*.

1.800.735.7323 • fax 612.337.5050 • help4kids@freespirit.com